ANIMAL SUPERPOWERS

AMAZING ANIMAL MOVERS

John Townsend

Raintree

Chicago, Illinois

www.capstonepub.com
Visit our website to find out more information about Heinemann-Raintree books.

To order:

☎ Phone 800-747-4992

🖥 Visit www.capstonepub.com
to browse our catalog and order online.

Edited by Rebecca Rissman, Dan Nunn, and Catherine Veitch
Designed by Joanna Hinton-Malivoire
Picture research by Mica Brancic
Production by Victoria Fitzgerald

Originated by Capstone Global Library
Printed and bound in China by CTPS

16 15 14 13 12
10 9 8 7 6 5 4 3 2 1

Library of Congress Cataloging-in-Publication Data
Townsend, John
Amazing animal movers / John Townsend.—1st ed.
p. cm.—(Animal superpowers)
Includes bibliographical references and index.
ISBN 978-1-4109-4746-8 (hb)
ISBN 978-1-4109-4753-6 (pb) 1. Animal locomotion—Juvenile literature. I. Title.
QP301.T67 2013
591.47′9—dc23   2011041356

Acknowledgments
We would like to thank the following for permission to reproduce photographs: Alamy pp. 12 (© WaterFrame), 23 (© Rolf Nussbaumer Photography), 11 (© Doug Perrine), 18 (© Mark Conlin); Corbis p. 13 (© Specialist Stock); FLPA p. 9 (Minden Pictures/Konrad Wothe); Getty Images pp. 10 (The Image Bank/Derek Berwin), 17 (Oxford Scientific/John Downer); Science Photo Library pp. 19 (John Shaw), 24 (Volker Steger); Shutterstock pp. 4 (© Danomyte), 5 (© Danshutter), 6 (© Mark Beckwith), 7 (© Marie Lumiere), 8 (© Sue Robinson), 14 (© Manja), 15 (© Chesapeake Images), 16 (© Netfalls), 20 (© Arto Hakola), 25 (© Eric Isselée), 26 (© Catmando), 27 (© Josef78), 29 (© Danomyte); p. 22 (© Photoshot).

Cover photograph of a basilisk lizard, Costa Rica, reproduced with permission of Nature Picture Library (© Bence Mate).

Every effort has been made to contact copyright holders of material reproduced in this book. Any omissions will be rectified in subsequent printings if notice is given to the publisher.

We would like to thank Michael Bright for his invaluable help in the preparation of this book.

Disclaimer
All the Internet addresses (URLs) given in this book were valid at the time of going to press. However, due to the dynamic nature of the Internet, some addresses may have changed, or sites may have changed or ceased to exist since publication. While the author and publisher regret any inconvenience this may cause readers, no responsibility for any such changes can be accepted by either the author or the publisher.

Some words are shown in bold, **like this**. You can find out what they mean by looking in the glossary.

Contents

Animals Can Be Superheroes!

Have you ever wanted superpowers? Your body is amazing, but you need to move extra-fast and far to be a superhero. Many animals do just that. Read this book to find out which animals use superpowers for super-travel.

Did You Know?

A spine-tailed swift can fly more than 100 miles per hour (mph). That is super-fast!

Super Speed on Land

A cheetah can speed from 0 to 60 miles per hour (mph) in less than 3 seconds. That is faster than many sports cars. This super-cat can run at nearly 70 mph to catch its **prey**.

small head and **sleek** shape for speed

bendable spine for huge strides

long, strong legs for super-**thrust**

7

Super Speed in the Air

The peregrine falcon is the fastest bird on the planet. It **soars** to a great height and then dives for its **prey**. Its body changes shape, and it slices through the air like a dart.

Did You Know?
Peregrine falcons can dive at speeds of about 200 mph!

Super Speed in Water

The sailfish is not much bigger than a human, but it is so much faster! It folds its **fins** close to its body so that it slips smoothly through the sea. For short bursts, a sailfish can reach nearly 70 mph. This makes it the fastest fish in the ocean.

Sailfish raise their sail-fins on their backs when they hunt together and round up small fish.

Super Speed in and out of Water

A flying fish swims at super-fast speed before it flies out of the sea. Its thin, wing-like **fins** allow it to jump and glide more than 3 feet above the waves for up to 650 feet at a time. That is the length of four Olympic-sized swimming pools!

Did You Know?
Flying fish can **soar** high enough to land on the decks of ships!

Super Flight

Hummingbirds' wings can beat up to 90 times per second. That means they can hover in midair like a helicopter. What powers their amazing energy is the sweet **nectar** from flowers that they sip every few minutes. They also eat tiny insects, for **protein**.

Did You Know?

Hummingbirds are the only birds that can fly backward.

Super High

Imagine being able to fly above the highest mountains in the world. Some birds can do just that. The griffon vulture is the world's highest-flying bird. It has been spotted seven miles up in the sky.

Bar-headed geese have been seen flying about five miles up in the sky!

Did You Know?

Bar-headed geese can fly higher than Mount Everest.

Super Far

Many animals spend their lives on the move to find food or safe places to raise their young. This is called **migration**. Salmon can remember the smell of their "home river," even after being away at sea for years.

As salmon swim upstream, they may even leap up waterfalls to reach safe places to lay their eggs.

Terrific Trip

The truly amazing **Arctic** tern flies more than 44,000 miles every year from the Arctic to the **Antarctic** and back again. Partway into their journey, these birds stop to feed. This fuels them for their **migration** all the way across the world.

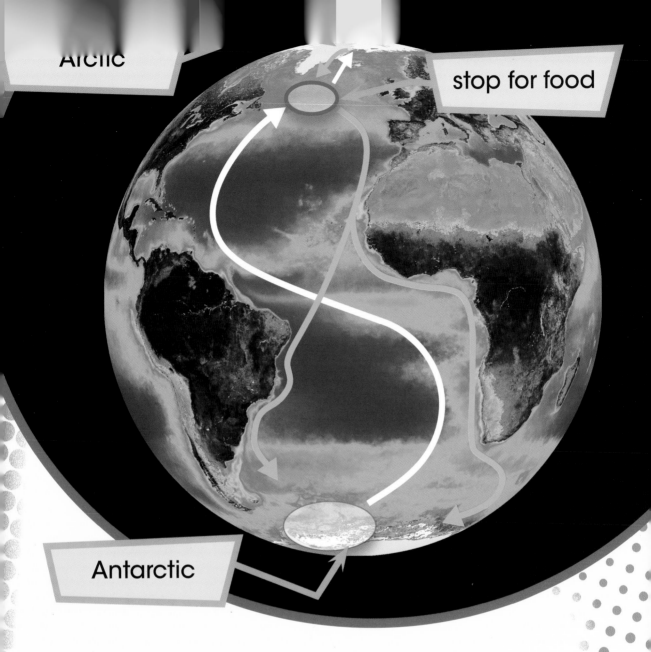

Arctic

stop for food

Antarctic

After setting out from the Arctic
(the top yellow line above), terns
feed on fish (in the red circle), then
fly south to the Antarctic. Then they
follow the winds back (the white line).

Super Move

A basilisk lizard can run over water! Its large back feet trap air under them, so it actually runs on little pockets of air on top of water. The lizard has to keep running fast, or the air bubble will burst before it takes the next step. If that happened, the lizard would sink.

back foot

23

Super Toes

Another tiny lizard has a different superpower for moving around. The gecko has special toe suction, so it can climb up walls, glass, and even across ceilings. Tiny hairs on each of its toes can stick to almost any surface.

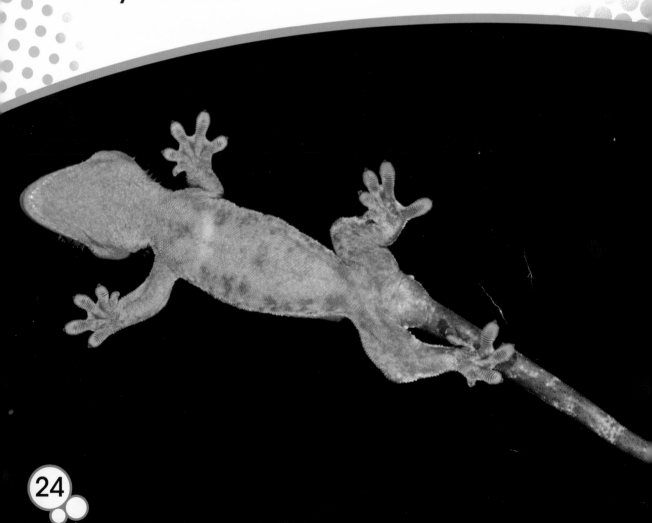

Did You Know?

Scientists are making **fabric** and robots to work like gecko feet. Firefighters may soon be able to climb up buildings for their work!

Terrific Travel

Whales are always on the move through the oceans. These humpback whales travel huge distances. How do they find their way in dark or murky water? It seems their brains have built-in maps to guide them!

Did You Know?

The gray whale swims more than 5,500 miles in 90 days, twice a year.

Quiz: Spot the Superhero!

Test your powers of observation and see if you can spot the superhero. You can find the answers on page 32, if you are really stuck!

1. Which of these animals can run the fastest?
a) a horse
b) a cheetah
c) an ostrich

2. Which of these animals can skydive the fastest?
a) a goose
b) a peregrine falcon
c) a tern

3. Which of these animals can swim
the fastest?
a) a hummingbird
b) a whale
c) a sailfish

4. Which of these animals can fly
the highest?
a) a bar-headed goose
b) a hummingbird
c) a basilisk lizard

5. Which of these animals can travel
the farthest?
a) a gecko
b) a tern
c) a cheetah

Glossary

Antarctic area around the South Pole of Earth

Arctic area around the North Pole of Earth

fabric type of cloth

fin part of a fish that helps it to swim

migration movement from one area to another over long distances

nectar sweet liquid found in flowers that is food for some insects and birds

prey animal that is hunted by other animals for food

protein important part of a diet, found in meat and other foods, which helps body growth and repair

sleek smooth

soar fly high up into the air

thrust force that allows something to move forward

Find Out More

Books

Costain, Meredith. *My Life in the Wild: Cheetah* (Animal Planet). New York: Kingfisher, 2011.

Gilpin, Daniel. *Record-Breaking Animals* (Record Breakers). New York: PowerKids, 2012.

Johnson, Jinny. *Amazing Animals* (Explorers). New York: Kingfisher, 2012.

Websites

pbskids.org/dragonflytv/show/cheetahs.html
This Website has a video about cheetahs.

video.nationalgeographic.com/video/player/ animals/birds-animals/birds-of-prey/falcon_ peregrine_velocity.html
Watch a speed test of a peregrine falcon on this Website. (You may need to watch an advertisement before the peregrine falcon video begins.)

video.nationalgeographic.com/video/player/ kids/animals-pets-kids/birds-kids/hummingbird- kids.html
See a video about hummingbirds.

Index

Answers: 1.b, 2.b, 3.c, 4.a, 5.b.